KUBLA KHAN

ALAN RAWSTHORNE

Kubla Khan

for contralto and tenor soli, chorus, and orchestra

orchestrated by
Edward Harper

vocal score

MUSIC DEPARTMENT

OXFORD
UNIVERSITY PRESS

OXFORD
UNIVERSITY PRESS

Great Clarendon Street, Oxford OX2 6DP, England
198 Madison Avenue, New York, NY 10016, USA

Oxford University Press is a department of the University of Oxford.
It furthers the University's aim of excellence in research, scholarship,
and education by publishing worldwide

Oxford is a registered trade mark of Oxford University Press
in the UK and in certain other countries

1 3 5 7 9 10 8 6 4 2

ISBN 978-0-19-335930-7

Music and text origination by Roger Turner
Printed in Great Britain on acid-free paper by
Halstan & Co. Ltd., Amersham, Bucks.

Orchestrator's Note

In 1940 the flat in Bristol where Alan Rawsthorne and his wife were staying was destroyed in a bombing raid on the city. Fortunately they were unhurt, but several manuscripts were lost, including the score of *Kubla Khan*. This had been written as part of a joint commission for exchange broadcasts between the BBC and Swiss Radio (the Swiss work was Honegger's oratorio *La Danse des Morts*). The Honegger was broadcast in April 1940 and the Rawsthorne two months later. The destruction of the manuscript and the absence of any recording meant that all that survived of the work was the vocal score used for the BBC broadcast. Rawsthorne was never persuaded to reconstruct the full score, but his response to Coleridge's poem—'this extraordinary burst of sustained genius', as he described it—is fascinating, and when John Turner, on behalf of the Ida Carroll Trust and with the support of the Rawsthorne Trust, asked me to consider orchestrating *Kubla Khan* I was very pleased to do so.

I was aware that Rawsthorne's original scoring had been for strings and percussion. However, the more I got to know the orchestral reduction the more I felt that parts of the music seemed to call for rather larger forces and a greater range of orchestral colour (John McCabe reaches a similar conclusion in his book on Rawsthorne). Furthermore, Rawsthorne had himself rescored the original version of his Piano Concerto No. 1 (like *Kubla Khan* it had been for strings and percussion) for full orchestra. This example of the composer himself rethinking his material for full orchestra provided me with a model for what I felt would be needed in the treatment of *Kubla Khan*. Such an undertaking as this requires a certain amount of imagination and creative freedom, but it has not been my intention that this should in any way reflect my own musical personality. My approach is close to Gordon Jacob's orchestration of the Elgar G major Organ Sonata where, in listening to it, I certainly would assume it to be Elgar's own work. Without claiming to write what Rawsthorne might have done himself, I hope to have found an orchestral sound which will do justice to this fine work.

EDWARD HARPER
June 2006

The re-orchestration by Edward Harper of Alan Rawsthorne's *Kubla Khan* was commissioned by the Ida Carroll Trust. The preparation of performing material has been made possible by the co-operation of the Rawsthorne Trust and through a generous contribution by the Ida Carroll Trust.

Instrumentation

3 flutes (3rd doubling piccolo)
2 oboes
2 clarinets in B flat
2 bassoons

4 horns in F
3 trumpets in C
2 tenor trombones
bass trombone
tuba

timpani
percussion (3 players: xylophone, tambourine, cymbals, suspended cymbal, whip, side drum, tenor drum, and bass drum)

harp
strings

Performing material is available on hire from the publisher's hire library.

Duration: *c.*16 mins

Metronome marks are editorial suggestions only, and appear in square brackets. Rawsthorne's original vocal score does not contain metronome marks.

KUBLA KHAN

Samuel Taylor Coleridge

Alan Rawsthorne

OXFORD UNIVERSITY PRESS, MUSIC DEPARTMENT, GREAT CLARENDON STREET, OXFORD OX2 6DP

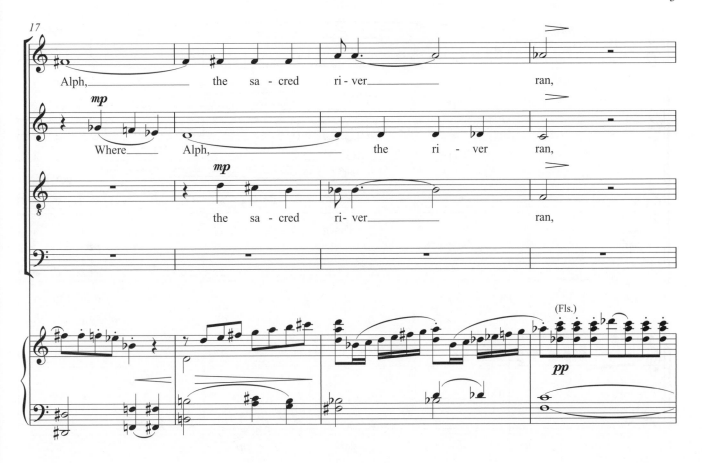

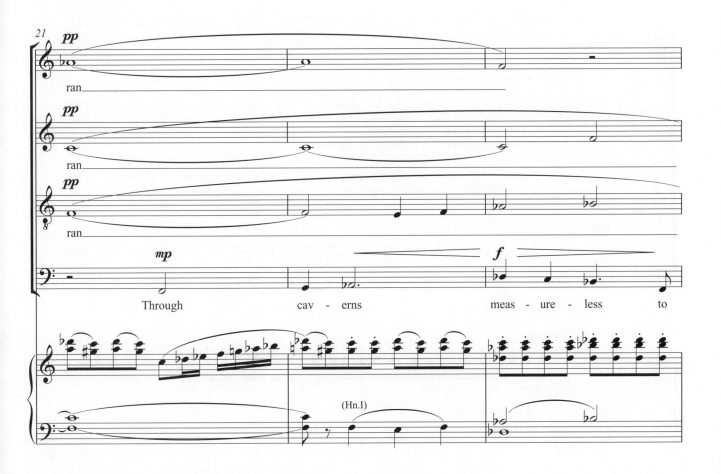

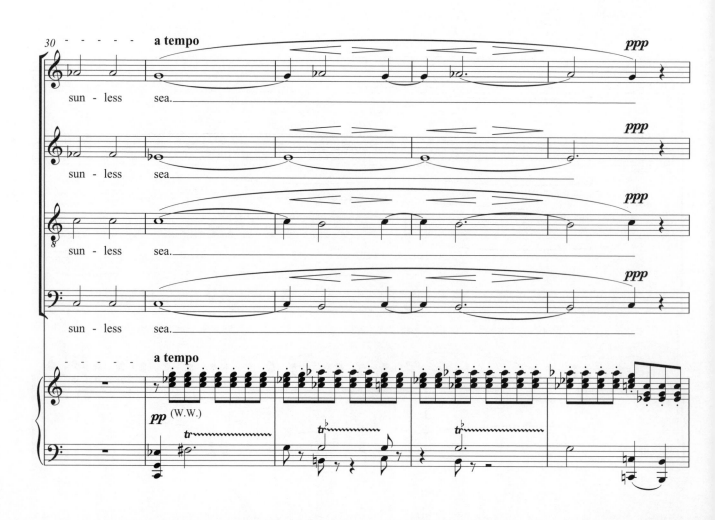

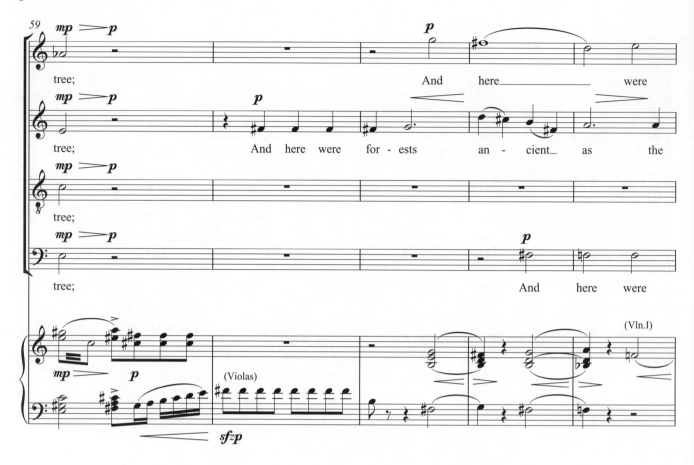

-fold - ing sun - ny spots of green-er - y.

-fold - ing sun - ny spots of green-er - y.

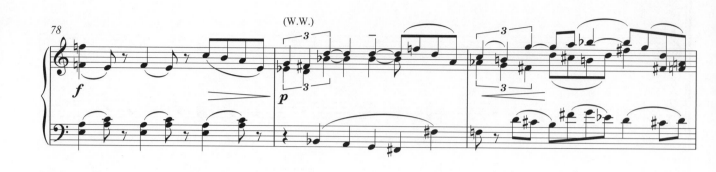

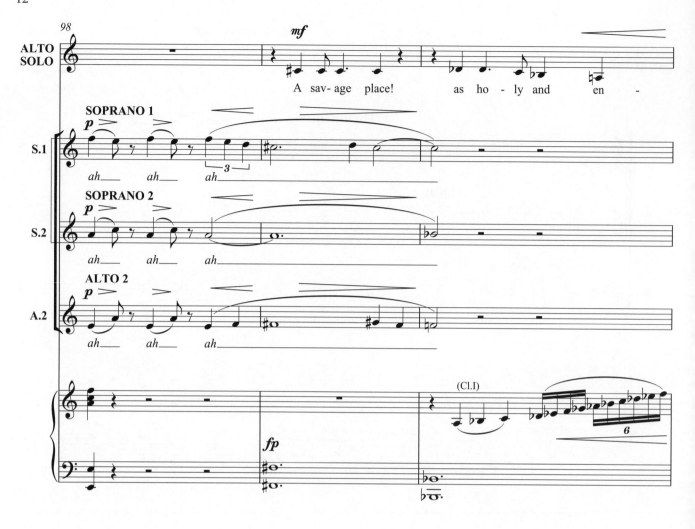

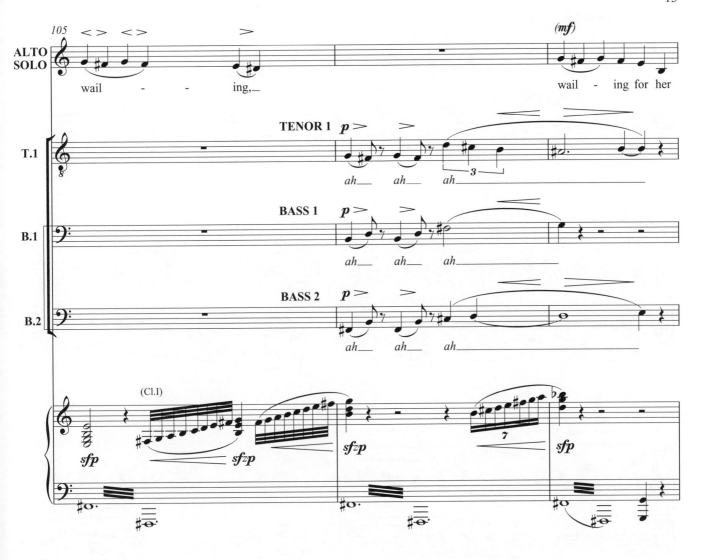

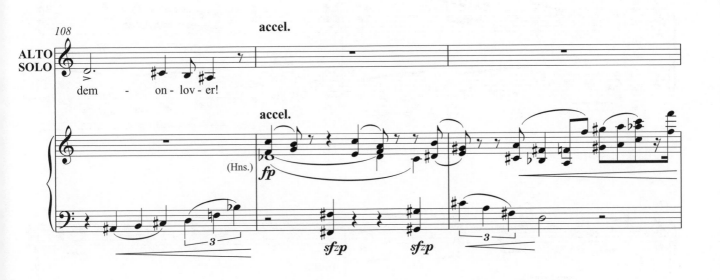

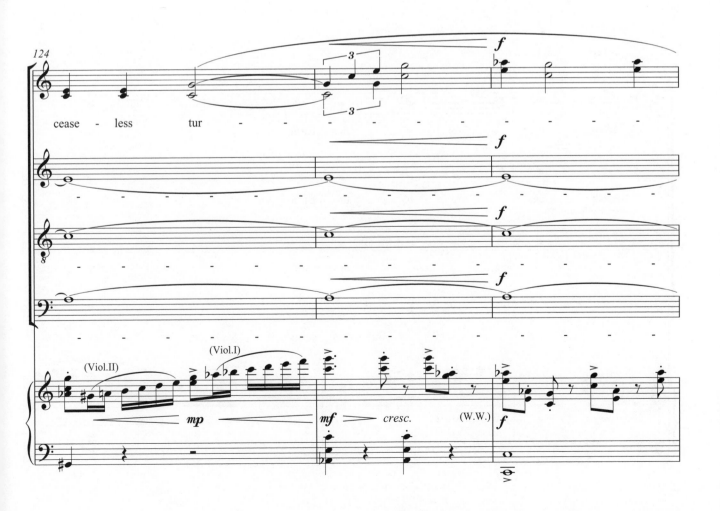

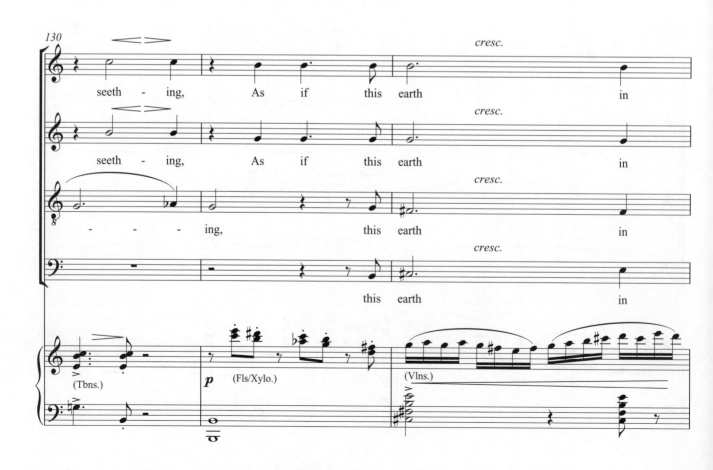

fast thick pants were breath - - - ing,
fast thick pants were breath - - ing,
fast thick pants were breath - - ing,
fast thick pants were breath - - - ing,

(Brass)

A might - y foun - tain mo - - ment -
A might - y foun - tain mo - - ment -
A might - - y foun - tain mo - ment -
A might - y foun -

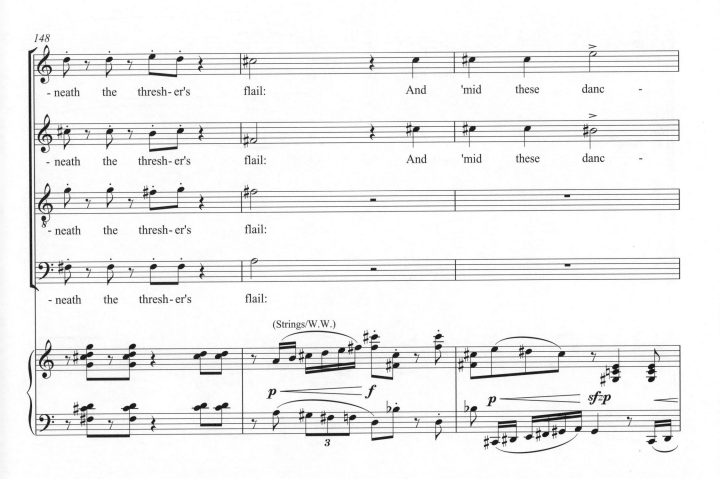

151

-ing rocks at once and ev - - - er It

-ing rocks at once and ev - - - er It

(W.W.)

fp

154

flung up mo - ment - ly the sa - - - - - -

p

flung up mo - ment - ly the sa - - - - - -

p

f *p* *f* *p*

(Strings) *cresc.*

p

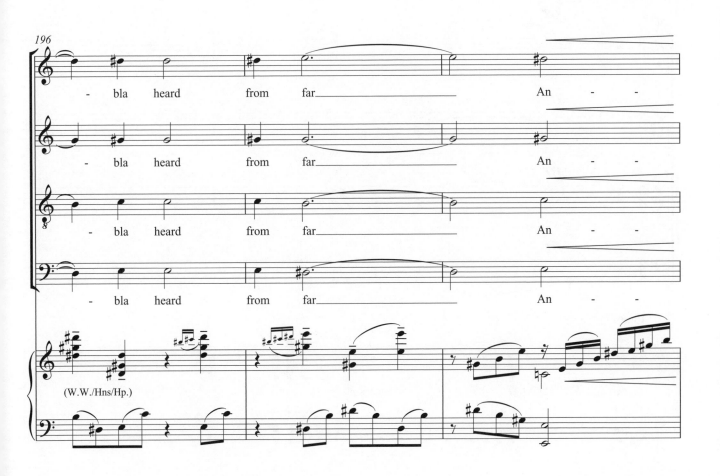

27

The sha- dow of the dome of pleas-ure Float - ed on the

The sha- dow of the dome of pleas-ure of the dome,_____

pleas-ure, The sha- dow of the dome of pleas-ure,

pleas-ure, The sha- dow of the dome of pleas-ure, of the dome,_____

(W.W./Hp.)

waves;_____

p

From the foun -

p

Where was heard_____ the ming - led meas-ure From the foun -

p

From the

L.H.

p (Strings)

(Fl.I/Hp.)

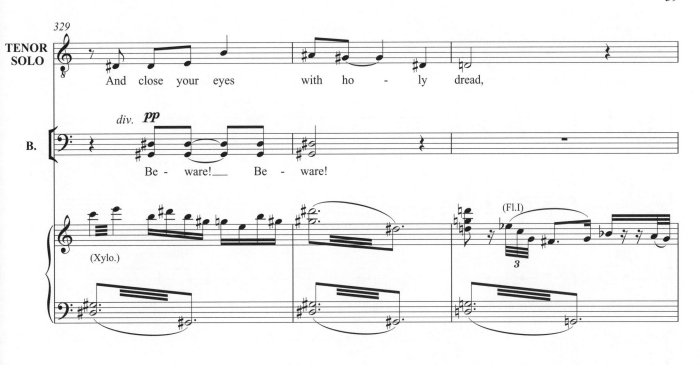

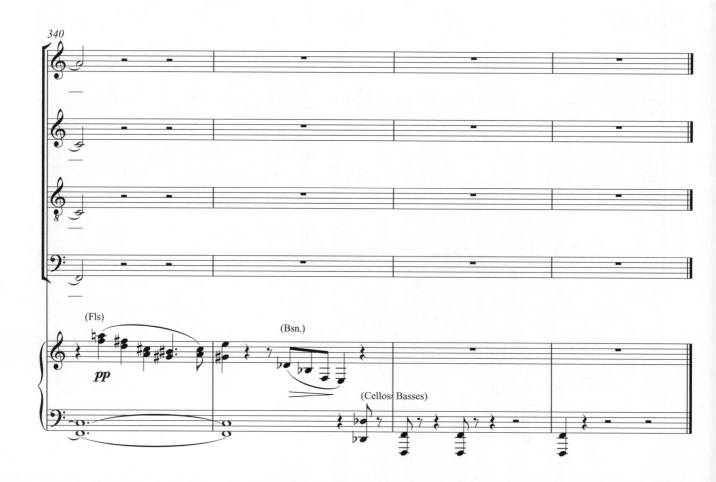